I HATE NOTRE DAME
303 Reasons Why You Should, Too

Crane Hill
PUBLISHERS
BIRMINGHAM, ALABAMA
1995

I HATE NOTRE DAME
303 Reasons Why You Should, Too

by Paul Finebaum

CRANE HILL
PUBLISHERS

Copyright 1995 by Paul Finebaum

All rights reserved
Printed in the United States of America
Published by Crane Hill Publishers
First edition, first printing

Library of Congress Cataloging-in-Publication Data

Finebaum, Paul, 1955-
  I hate Notre Dame : 303 reasons why you should, too / by Paul Finebaum. -- 1st ed.
    p.   cm.
  ISBN 1-881548-77-5
  1. University of Notre Dame--Football--Miscellanea. 2. Notre Dame Fighting Irish (Football team) -- Miscellanea. I. Title.
GV958.N6F55   1995
796.332'63'0977289--dc20   95-34955
                                                                     CIP

10   9   8   7   6   5   4   3   2   1

I HATE NOTRE DAME

I Hate Notre Dame Because…

1. The crap about the Four Horsemen.

2. The classless manner in which the school handled Gerry Faust.

3. The fact that the school was stupid enough to hire a high school coach in the first place.

4. The fact that the school was stupid enough to believe Lou Holtz was cleaner than the driven snow.

5. The way the school handled the dismissal of Digger Phelps.

6. The way it permits Lou Holtz to berate and rough up officials.

7. The way it passes itself off as an academic institution when it really is nothing more than a football factory.

8. The way it lies about steroid use.

9. The way it lies about academic standards.

10. The way it promotes violence.

11. The way it condones trash-talking.

12. The way it plays injured athletes.

13. The deplorable, despicable manner in which it misled the CFA while negotiating its own television package with NBC.

14. The manner in which it acts more like a banking institution than an academic institution.

15. The myth about Notre Dame comebacks. For example, Notre Dame blowing a 24-point lead against Stanford before losing 36-31.

16. Blowing a 24-point lead against Tennessee in 1991 before losing 35-34.

17. Blowing the Michigan game in 1992 that ended in a tie.

18. Blowing the Stanford game in 1992 after leading by 16 at home.

19. Blowing the national championship in the waning moments against Boston College in 1993.

20. Blowing the Michigan game in the final seconds in 1994.

21. The hottest bumper sticker at coaching conventions in the future will probably be, "Honk if you haven't come from behind to beat a Lou Holtz-coached team."

22. Former quarterback Tony Rice was admitted to Notre Dame by getting three letters of his first name and two of his second correct on the application.

23. Lou Holtz watches old videos of Woody Hayes to help improve his headlock position on officials.

24. If Holtz ever writes another book, a good idea for a title might be, *All the Different Ways I've Blown the Boston College Game.*

25. It was Lou Holtz who once said he didn't mind playing in a bowl on Christmas Day because "after going to church and opening up the gifts…Christmas is a very boring day."

26. Knute Rockne would roll over in his grave if he could see some of Holtz's antics.

27. The Leprechaun is the dumbest mascot in college sports.

28. The men at Notre Dame have so little understanding of pretty women that posters of "The Fabulous Sports Babe" are often seen on the walls of dorm rooms.

29. Rudy could have probably started on the 1994 team.

30. The movie *The Day the World Ended* is about Notre Dame's annual game with Boston College.

31. Lou Holtz declared a national day of celebration when Gary Moeller resigned at Michigan.

32. Since they are so popular, Notre Dame officials ought to consider putting steroid dispensers in the football locker room.

33. Notre Dame fans believe the bumper sticker "And on the Seventh Day, God created the Fighting Irish" to be accurate.

34. Fans think only two people have walked on water and one of them coached at Notre Dame.

35. It is a good thing Notre Dame fans don't have to pass an IQ test to become season ticket holders.

36. Joe Montana wrote his senior thesis at Notre Dame on the best way to keep a skunk from smelling. His solution: hold the skunk's nose.

37. Joe Montana is living proof you don't need a three digit IQ to get a degree from ND.

38. Frank Gifford considered going to Notre Dame instead of USC, until he found out they let in wimps like Regis.

39. Regis Philbin's new workout video "Under the Golden Dome" features Lou Holtz and the dancing leprechauns.

40. Regis was so poor he went to communion four or five times a day just to eat the wafers.

41. Regis never met a chili dog he didn't like.

42. Notre Dame's home economics department has a course called "Polish Gourmet Cooking."

43. The Notre Dame business school has a course titled "Managing a 7-11."

44. The FDA is considering allowing motivational speeches by Tony Roberts to become legal replacements for sleeping pills.

45. Lou Holtz is so cheap he once took a free visit to Dr. Kevorkian.

46. John MacLoed promised to turn the ND program around quickly. He has done so by taking the school from mediocrity to oblivion in a short time.

47. Regis recently finished his last book. At least, people hope it is.

48. Someone once put it best when he said, "I know they bend the rules up there, but I was watching a game between Notre Dame and Michigan when they started the game with a burglar alarm."

49. Notre Dame broadcaster Tom Pagna has been spotted downtown wearing the sign, "Will broadcast for food."

50. Notre Dame has a graduate course called "How to avoid marrying your next of kin."

51. The Irish have a graduate school for belching.

52. Notre Dame fans think the book *The End of Time* was about the day Gerry Faust arrived in South Bend.

53. Some school fans think "007" refers to the GPA of the Irish football team.

54. Lee Becton once said, "Class, what class? Coach Holtz never said anything about me doing schoolwork."

55. Paul Horning once asked to change his major at Notre Dame. He told the dean he thought physical education was just too hard.

56. An academic All-American at Notre Dame is someone who goes to class once a semester.

57. Notre Dame fans talk about rebuilding after a two-loss season.

58. Considering all the money doled out to Notre Dame players, the school should think about joining the NFC Central Division.

59. Regis used to think the four horsemen ran in the Kentucky Derby.

60. Bobby Taylor believes "Planet Reebok" is the planet right before Pluto.

61. Some Notre Dame history professors claim the book *War and Peace* was about the relationship between Lou Holtz and Frank Broyles.

62. A group of Notre Dame seniors was recently asked to vote on the top choices for commencement speaker. Pee Wee Herman finished first.

63. Mike Tyson finished second.

64. Paul Finebaum finished third.

65. Regis went swimming in Loch Ness and the monster got out.

66. Lee Becton said he considered majoring in journalism at Notre Dame because he was bored with physical education.

67. Holtz is so slow he thinks Jenny Craig is a former homecoming queen.

68. Tony Rice said the reason he didn't want to play for the CFL is that he didn't enjoy traveling overseas.

69. Notre Dame players wear Nike shoes on dates, hoping their girlfriends will say, "Just do it."

70. Lou Holtz can say absolutely nothing and mean it.

71. Notre Dame fans refuse to visit Mount Rushmore because Knute Rockne's face isn't featured.

72. Joe Montana actually believes the state was named after him.

73. Dick Rosenthal always has two seats in the athletic director's box, one for himself and one for his ego.

74. Notre Dame cheerleaders are tested weekly for makeup poisoning.

75. Favorite pickup line for Notre Dame players, "Didn't we almost flunk out together?"

76. Irish football players are not required to go the library before they graduate; however, they must learn how to spell it.

77. If Roger Valdiserri died during a football game, how would anyone know?

78. *The Odd Couple* was the real-life story of Lou Holtz and Dick Rosenthal.

79. Notre Dame fans think Armageddon is if Northwestern ever beats the Irish in football.

80. Lou Holtz has a hard time making enemies at Notre Dame because his friends hate him so much.

81. You can always tell when it's finals time in South Bend. That's usually when the football team buys the books.

82. Notre Dame Stadium has to put in a new smoke detector every time the ND cheerleaders drop by because their perfume sets off the device.

83. The following is a list of the 10 biggest wimps to graduate from Notre Dame: Regis.

84. Regis.

85. Regis.

I HATE NOTRE DAME

86. Regis.

87. Regis.

88. Regis.

89. Regis.

90. Regis.

91. Regis.

92. Regis.

93. Lou Holtz has a Venus flytrap in his mouth because it is always open.

94. Lee Becton was ND's nomination for the academic All-American last year when he spelled his name correctly and got the date right.

95. The common belief on campus is that the ABC series *Coach* is based on the real-life story of Gerry Faust.

96. Regis never could understand the difference between lent and lint.

97. Bug zappers with Lou Holtz's picture on them are hot Christmas items this year.

98. Lou Holtz is so cheap he deducts charitable contributions to the widow of the unknown soldier.

99. The toughest thing Rick Mirer ever tried to do at Notre Dame was out talk Lou Holtz.

100. Holtz is such an optimist he actually looked forward to getting married.

101. A poll of Notre Dame fans revealed the top 10 men they most wanted their sons to be like: Bill Bilinski.

102. Mike Tyson.

103. Danny Sheridan.

104. Ronald McDonald.

105. Ron Lesko.

106. Joe Kuherich.

107. Kato Kaelin.

108. Bo Jackson.

109. Michael Jackson.

110. Milli Vanilli.

111. Lee Becton once said, "Notre Dame football is great because you get to bite, kick, scratch, fight, get sweaty, and afterwards hug a blond."

112. Bill Clinton decided not to go to Notre Dame after he learned they couldn't have sex before marriage.

113. South Bend is such a hick town the picture postcards are blank.

114. Tony Roberts' favorite drink is Rolaids and Perrier.

115. The hotels are so bad near the Irish campus that to get room service you have to dial 911.

116. Tony Rice once said, "If we didn't have to go to class, this really would be a cool school."

117. Lou Holtz can say less in more time than any human being in the world.

118. Skip Holtz said the happiest day of his life was when he left Notre Dame for UConn.

119. Networks are considering banning Notre Dame games because there is too much violence between Lou Holtz and the officials.

120. Even though Notre Dame deserved the national championship in 1994 over FSU, Holtz's whining made even his closest friends want to puke.

121. During freshman orientation, the school has a course for athletes called "Brushing your teeth."

122. Counting to 500 is a requirement for the Rhodes Scholar candidates from Notre Dame.

123. *Playboy* featured a Leprechaun in its series "Girls of Notre Dame" because it couldn't find a good-looking coed.

124. The most feared words for any Notre Dame cheerleader are, "Sorry, honey, we just ran out of bacon."

125. A romantic date for a Notre Dame coed is going to Bob Evans' breakfast bar.

126. Last year's homecoming queen was so ugly that when they took her to the top of the Golden Dome, she was attacked by a plane.

127. After reading Lou Holtz's autobiography, one critic wrote, "Once you put down one of his books, you can't pick it up again."

128. Tom Pagna is so dull he lights up a room when he leaves it.

129. There is something to be said for Holtz and he is usually saying it.

130. The Notre Dame campus doesn't need a Comedy Club. All the students have to do for a laugh is watch the Notre Dame basketball team.

131. Joey Buttafuoco has never missed a Notre Dame-USC game.

132. Notre Dame considered joining the Big East a few years back, but was afraid of a dirty word–competition.

133. After trailing at the half of the Michigan game, Holtz is reputed to have said, "If we lose, no matter what, I'll still love you and your mommas will still love you. But I can't make any promises about your girlfriends."

134. The only thing that could make the Notre Dame team happier than winning the national championship is if they made shoplifting legal.

135. Notre Dame didn't win the national championship last year, but led the nation in the number of players suspended.

136. ND fans think a honeymoon is when two fans bare their buttocks toward a public building.

137. Ara Parseghian is so old that when he was a teenager, the Dead Sea was still alive.

138. The most popular song on Notre Dame's campus among coeds is *Like a Virgin.*

139. It is almost as big of a joke as the football team's record last year.

140. Ron Powlus once said, "A mind is a terrible thing to waste. So I am donating mine to Notre Dame."

141. Some Notre Dame fans think a jock strap is a football player who's into S&M.

142. O.J. Simpson should have tried to escape to Notre Dame in 1994 because they would have never looked for a football player there.

143. A number of Notre Dame fans presume the leading rusher each year is a sorority sister who rushed the most girls.

144. They think higher education is when students have classes on the top floor of Hesburgh Library.

145. Some fans believe the Big Ten is the top 10 finalists in the Miss Notre Dame contest.

146. Tony Roberts once cracked open a bottle of champagne when he received a letter from Publisher's Clearing House saying he was a finalist for a million bucks.

147. Asked about manual labor in an economics class, Lee Becton answered that he was a great Mexican leader.

148. A number of Notre Dame fans are convinced Joe Paterno is related to Saddam Hussein.

149. John Hinckley's favorite pastime, other than dreaming of Jodie Foster, is listening to old tapes of Lindsey Nelson doing Notre Dame football.

150. John Hinckley is a Notre Dame fan.

151. Alumni think a Rhodes Scholar is a student traveling down Juniper Road.

152. Some followers of Notre Dame football think a Winnebago is a luxury car.

153. Lou Holtz fell in love with himself as a teenager. That way, he figured he wouldn't have any rivals.

154. John MacLoed may end up being to Notre Dame basketball what Gerry Faust was to the football program.

155. Outside the Notre Dame Stadium, a sign reads, "Bein' an idiot is no box of chocolates."

156. The three hardest words in the English language for an ND fan, "I was wrong."

157. ND football players get their early morning workouts by fighting for the toy in the Lucky Charms box.

158. The choice of car among football players at ND is a white Ford Bronco.

159. Dick Rosenthal is next on a waiting list for a charisma bypass.

160. Notre Dame graduates put their diplomas on their rear windows so they can park in handicap spaces.

161. Anthropologists have asked to see x-rays of Lou Holtz's skull for display at the National Museum.

162. Before declaring a major, freshmen at Notre Dame are also required to declare which is their favorite dancing raisin.

163. Gus Orenstein left Notre Dame last year because he couldn't find a good bagel in South Bend.

164. Lou Holtz is such an egomaniac he often gets upset at funerals because he's not the corpse.

165. The following is a list of Lou Holtz's favorite foods when he goes on a diet: Fried frog legs.

166. Chicken-fried steak.

167. Lightly-fried onion rings.

168. Gently-fried egg rolls.

169. Bob Evans' low-fat pecan log.

170. Stuckey's low-fat caramel brownies.

171. Goo-Goo Clusters with artificial sweetener.

172. Low-fat Vienna sausage.

173. Big Macs without the special sauce, cheese, and pickles.

174. French-fried cucumber sandwich.

175. The Irish coaching staff had to start separating Wives' Day and Girlfriends' Day because a couple of guys brought both.

176. Listening to Paul Horning talk about Irish football is the latest cure of insomnia in the Midwest.

177. Notre Dame's freshmen recently voted *The Price is Right* as their favorite television show because it reminded them of their recruitment.

178. The program *Let's Make a Deal* finished second.

179. Doug Looney is to Notre Dame football what Rush Limbaugh is to Bill Clinton.

180. The following are 10 words that many Notre Dame football players come to know well: Big House.

181. Joint.

182. Life without parole.

183. Making license plates.

184. Bend over and pick up the soap.

185. The chamber.

186. Chain gangs.

187. "No, warden, I wouldn't mind killing your wife in exchange for some time in the yard."

188. "No, I've never done that before."

189. "I'll trade you cigarettes for my national championship ring."

190. Dick Rosenthal has a pin-up of Fred Flintstone in his office.

191. The Notre Dame homecoming queen was so ugly she wore a turtleneck to cover her flea collar.

192. Notre Dame's communications school has a class in hosting segments of the Consumer Shopping Network.

193. Some Notre Dame students believe the book *How the Grinch Stole Christmas* is about the Notre Dame-BC series.

194. Holtz's mouth is so big, he can whisper in his own ear.

195. Holtz has gotten so old that his mind has gone from passion to pension.

196. The video of the Notre Dame-BC game from 1993 is not a big seller at the campus bookstore.

197. Rudy is to Notre Dame football what Barney Fife is to law enforcement.

198. For years Lou Holtz was an unknown failure. Now he is a known failure.

199. Doug Looney has no prejudices. He hates everyone at Notre Dame equally.

200. Some fans think the movie *Grumpy Old Men* is about the Notre Dame coaching staff.

201. Lou Holtz used to go to Julia Child for speech lessons.

202. Joe Montana donated the backseat of his car to the Notre Dame Sports Museum.

203. Notre Dame cheerleaders only like sex on days that have a "d" in them.

204. The best selling book in the Notre Dame campus store this winter will be *I hate Paul Finebaum*.

205. Regis is the kind of guy who goes to an orgy and complains about the cheese dip.

206. If Lee Corso and Lou Holtz went out to dinner, they would talk each other to death.

207. One of Holtz's favorite fantasies as a kid was being in a one-act play.

208. His favorite fantasy today is Michigan shutting down its football program.

209. South Bend isn't close to the end of the world, but you can sure see it from there.

210. Holtz's best joke is his record at the New York Jets.

211. Of all the songs ever recorded, the one Holtz hates the most is Simon & Garfunkel's "Sounds of Silence."

212. The only time Holtz is ever speechless is when someone asks him the last time he skipped a meal.

213. When Dick Rosenthal's doctor told him recently to eat more vegetables, he started putting two olives in every martini.

214. Tony Roberts favorite kind of party: "whine" and cheese.

215. John Heisler is so dull that when he goes to vote, they hand him an absentee ballot.

216. Holtz once told his wife, "I love you terribly." She said, "You sure do."

217. Asked once how his wife felt about his 18-hour days at ND, Holtz replied, "I don't know. I don't see her that much."

218. The movie *Forrest Gump* was modeled after the childhood of Lou Holtz.

219. The only reason Notre Dame won services to Ron Powlus was that Michigan got to the youngster's home after the bidding was closed.

220. The bumper sticker "Wait Until Next Year" has been the Notre Dame bookstore's hottest seller for a couple of years.

221. Lou and Beth Holtz have decided to take their vacation next spring on the Internet.

222. For his birthday, Holtz's wife, Beth, bought him the hot-selling book *The Pocket Guide to Better Sex* and told him to start reading.

223. Regis' biggest disappointment at Notre Dame was when he was rejected for the role of the Leprechaun.

224. Digger Phelps checked into a South Bend mental hospital last winter, complaining of "March Madness."

225. Holtz once said that marriage is the only war in which you sleep with the enemy.

226. Holtz is the only person known to man who can enter a room mouth-first.

227. Some Notre Dame coeds are so ugly that local restaurants hand them doggie bags before they eat.

228. Favorite movie among Notre Dame students last winter was *An Officer and his Genitals.*

229. The only good thing about South Bend is it's two hours away from Steve Dahl.

230. Lou Holtz has such a large ego he bows when it thunders.

231. Notre Dame has a rehabilitation hospital for students who are Hooked on Phonics.

232. The reason Notre Dame students look so upset at graduation is they now have to learn to spell the name of another city.

233. Notre Dame admission requirements for football players are 20 on the ACT and an IQ of 16.

234. Notre Dame has a special course for teaching the vice presidents since Quayle.

235. The Notre Dame infirmary has a course called "How to watch *Regis & Kathie Lee* without hurling."

236. Tim Brown once said he could have been a Rhodes Scholar except for the grades.

237. For an athlete to receive a degree from Notre Dame, he must be able to write his name, age, and social security number without making more than three mistakes.

238. Tim Brown once said, "I sure enjoyed winning the Heisman. But I am even more thankful they didn't ask me to spell it."

239. It is now mandatory for Notre Dame coeds to shave their underarms between April and June.

240. Notre Dame fans order *Sports Illustrated* for the free phone instead of for the swimsuit issue.

241. The food in some campus restaurants is so bad the only card they take is Blue Cross.

242. Brian Kato Kaelin once was a male cheerleader at Notre Dame.

243. Dick Rosenthal has a poster of Lisa Marie Presley and Michael Jackson on his bedroom wall.

244. Lou Holtz once said on his radio show that safe sex can only be practiced on top of a bank safe.

245. Tony Roberts once coined the phrase, "I was born at night. But it wasn't last night."

246. David Letterman considered going to Notre Dame until he found out they let in wimps like Regis.

247. Regis was so hard up for a date for homecoming that he asked out the Leprechaun.

248. When Lou Holtz was asked recently about the abortion bill, he responded, "Well, the first thing we should do is pay it."

249. Notre Dame fans were surprised to learn that the movie *From Here to Eternity* was about Pearl Harbor and not about trying to cope with Lou Holtz.

250. Beside the word "crass" in *Webster's Dictionary* is a picture of a Notre Dame fan.

251. Beano Cook once said racquetball was his favorite sport at ND. "I played yesterday for three hours and didn't lose a single ball."

252. Lou Holtz once yelled at his team at halftime of the ND-USC game, "What's wrong with you guys? You're playing like a bunch of amateurs."

253. Some Notre Dame coeds think intercourse is the time off between classes.

254. Notre Dame fans know the four seasons so well: football, football recruiting, cheating, and cheating some more.

255. Lou Holtz's brain is always fresh; he's never used it.

256. Holtz has a new book coming out next fall titled, *The 100 Biggest Games I Choked in.*

257. Notre Dame has toughened its entrance requirements. They now require you to type in your name on the form.

258. The South Bend airport would make a nice nuclear waste dump.

259. Lou Holtz's idea of Armageddon is being stuck on a desert island with Danny Sheridan and Beano Cook.

260. The tour guide for the city of South Bend is the loneliest job in town.

261. Holtz once told his staff, "I gave the sexual performance of my life last night. I'm just sorry my wife wasn't awake to see it."

262. Regis was so hard up for a date he once asked out one of the four horsemen.

263. Holtz once told a date, "Love at first sight saves a lot of time."

264. Holtz also said, "If you think looks improve with the years, try attending a class reunion."

265. Holtz often contradicts himself—and he is usually right.

266. Some Notre Dame seniors went ahead and enlisted last year instead of waiting for NFL draft day.

267. Holtz is in a class by himself, or should we say a lack of class all by himself.

268. Lou Holtz has willed his head to science. They are going to use it for an experimental rock garden.

269. Regis was so hard up for money that he once tried to sell birth control pills on campus.

270. Regis was so hard up for money that he once tried to open an abortion clinic on campus.

271. Regis was so hard up for money that he opened up a hot dog stand during lent.

272. Tony Roberts once said, "The best thing about football is that it only takes four quarters to finish a fifth."

273. South Bend is such a hick town the town hooker has to stand under a flashlight.

274. Holtz was so ugly at birth, his mother was arrested for littering.

275. Holtz was so ugly at birth, his doctor slapped his mother.

276. Holtz was so ugly at birth, his mother breast-fed him with a straw.

277. Raghib Ismail once said his fondest memory of Notre Dame was leaving it.

278. Digger Phelps still can't understand why the basketball arena wasn't named after him.

279. If Notre Dame dropped their basketball program, would anybody notice?

280. After five games last season, Dick Rosenthal said, "If lessons are learned in defeat, as they say, our team is really getting a great education."

281. Notre Dame cheerleaders don't like to lie out in the summer because the heat might melt their plastic surgery.

282. Roger Valdiserri has a secret fetish for Betty Crocker.

283. Some Notre Dame cheerleaders are so ugly they are often mistaken for circus animals.

284. Some of the cheerleaders were said to be uglier than sin. That was, until sin sued.

285. If a national championship were awarded for having the drunkest fans, Notre Dame would retire the trophy.

286. As well as for having the most obnoxious fans.

287. Gerry Faust left Notre Dame several years ago complaining of illness and fatigue. The fans were sick and tired of him.

288. O.J. Simpson considered Notre Dame over USC until he heard they were already over the salary cap.

289. Roger Valdiserri is so old he handled public relations for Lewis & Clark's expedition.

290. Dick Rosenthal is believed to have said, "Our society doesn't need to get rid of our coaches. Instead, we need to find a way to get rid of the alumni."

291. Beth Holtz once said, "People ask me to speak about various topics. I always promise I will speak about sex and marriage, but being Lou's wife, I don't know anything about either."

292. Success hasn't gone to Lou Holtz's head. Just to his mouth.

293. The next time Lou Holtz mentions high class recruits, try mentioning this name: Michael Miller.

294. Notre Dame has a business course for football players called "How to steal a VCR."

295. The captain of the cheerleading squad is determined by which girl has the smallest fever blister.

296. Followers of the Notre Dame program think *America's Most Wanted* is about their football team.

297. Regis was so hard up for money that he sold rosary beads outside of Notre Dame Stadium.

298. One book Lou Holtz apparently has never read is an NCAA rules manual.

299. What is blue and gold, 100 yards long, and has two front teeth? The front row at the Notre Dame Stadium.

300. Holtz has instituted a "Don't ask, don't tell" policy among recruits.

301. Regis tried to meet Notre Dame women coming out of confession.

302. Valdiserri quit gambling after the Civil War. He had the South plus the points.

303. The Leprechaun had to be spayed before last season.